HISTORY & GEOGRAPHY 404
GRASSLANDS

Author:
Theresa K. Buskey, B.A., J.D.

Editor:
Alan Christopherson, M.S.

Assistant Editor:
Annette M. Walker, B.S.

Media Credits:
Page 3: © tycoon751, iStock, Thinkstock; **5:** © tycoon751, iStock, Thinkstock; **9:** © Gary Tognoni, iStock, Thinkstock; **10:** © MattiaATH, iStock, Thinkstock; **15:** © Photos.com, Thinkstock; **17:** © Photos.com, Thinkstock; **19:** © demerzel21, iStock, Thinkstock; **21:** © toniton, iStock, Thinkstock; **26:** © NiseriN, iStock, Thinkstock; **27:** © Anup Shah, Digital Vision, Thinkstock; **30:** © ClaraNila, iStock, Thinkstock; **32:** © Andrea Purmann, iStock, Thinkstock; **34:** © Alexander Kuguchin, iStock, Thinkstock; **35:** (left) © Georgios Kollidas, Hemera, Thinkstock; **37:** © JJS-Pepite, iStock, Thinkstock; **38:** © Anup Shah, Digital Vision, Thinkstock; **40:** © Robin Camarote, iStock, Thinkstock; **45:** © Ekaterina Krasnikova, iStock, Thinkstock; **48:** © diegorayaces, iStock, Thinkstock; **49:** © Edsel Querini, iStock, Thinkstock; **51:** © javarman3, iStock, Thinkstock; **53:** © pascalou95, iStock, Thinkstock; **55:** © Frizi, iStock, Thinkstock; **56:** © Dorling Kindersley, Thinkstock; **57:** © klausbalzano, iStock, Thinkstock; **58:** © Mike Watson Images, moodboard, Thinkstock.

Alpha Omega
PUBLICATIONS

804 N. 2nd Ave. E.
Rock Rapids, IA 51246-1759

LIFEPAC®

HISTORY & GEOGRAPHY

STUDENT BOOK

▶ **4th Grade** | Unit 4

Alpha Omega
PUBLICATIONS

GRASSLANDS

There are four important areas of plant life in the world. They are forests, tundras, deserts, and grasslands. The grasslands are drier than the forests, warmer than the tundras, and wetter than the deserts. They are an especially important region to people.

Of the four areas, the grasslands are the best for growing food, for several reasons. Grasslands are usually flat, or nearly flat, which makes them easy to farm. The soil is usually very good for crops. Moreover, quite a bit more than half of the food people grow to feed themselves <u>is</u> grass. Wheat, rice, corn, barley, millet, and sugar cane are all grasses. It makes sense that these crops grow well in areas where wild grasses grow. Thus, grasslands are very important to people.

In this **LIFEPAC®** you will study grasslands and three grassland countries. You will learn about the plants and animals of the grasslands. You will also study the Ukraine in Europe, Kenya in Africa, and Argentina in South America. You will learn about how the grasslands have been a part of those countries and their history.

Objectives

Read these objectives. The objectives tell you what you will be able to do when you have successfully completed this LIFEPAC. Each section will list according to the numbers below what objectives will be met in that section. When you have finished this LIFEPAC, you should be able to:

1. Name and identify the different grasslands.
2. Explain why grasslands are important and where they are located.
3. Explain the geography, history, people, and life today in the three grassland countries.
4. Explain how the grasslands affected the countries you study.
5. Tell some of the products of the grassland countries.

1. UKRAINE

This section of the LIFEPAC will teach you about the many grasslands all over the world. You will learn some of their names, the animals that live on them, and where they are. Then, you will study the country of Ukraine, which is located in eastern Europe on the grasslands of Eurasia. It is a new country that was created when the Soviet Union split apart in 1991. But the land is old, even if the country is new. You will learn about both.

Objectives

Review these objectives. When you have completed this section, you should be able to:

1. Name and identify the different grasslands.
2. Explain why grasslands are important and where they are located.
3. Explain the geography, history, people, and life today in the three grassland countries.
4. Explain how the grasslands affected the countries you study.
5. Tell some of the products of the grassland countries.

Vocabulary

Study these new words. Learning the meanings of these words is a good study habit and will improve your understanding of this LIFEPAC.

autocratic (ô tə krat′ ik). Having absolute power; ruling without limits.

bauxite (bôk′ sīt). A mineral from which aluminum is obtained.

communism (kom′ yə niz′ əm). A system in which most or all property is owned by the state and is shared by all.

dairy (dār′ ē). Having to do with milk and products made from milk.

embroidery (em broi′ dər ē). Ornamental designs sewn in cloth or leather with a needle.

expose (ek spōz'). To lay open; uncover; leave without protection.

famine (fam' ən). A lack of food in a place; a time of starving.

fertile (fėr' təl). Able to produce much; producing crops easily.

flax (flaks). A slender, upright plant. Its seeds are used for linseed oil, and linen is made from its stems.

herbivore (hėr' bə vôr). Plant-eating animal.

manganese (mang' gə nēz). A hard, brittle grayish-white metal used in making steel.

nuclear (nü' klē ər). Of or having to do with atomic energy or atomic weapons.

peasant (pez' ənt). A farmer of the working class in Europe.

persecution (pėr' sə kyü' shən). Being treated badly, especially because of one's beliefs.

serf (sėrf). A slave who could not be sold off the land, but passed from one owner to another with the land.

titanium (tī tā' nē əm). A lightweight, strong metal that has many uses including airplanes, tools, and armor plate.

uranium (yù rā' nē əm). A heavy, white, radioactive metal used as a source of atomic energy.

Note: *All vocabulary words in this LIFEPAC appear in* **boldface** *print the first time they are used. If you are unsure of the meaning when you are reading, study the definitions given.*

Pronunciation Key: hat, āge, cãre, fär; let, ēqual, tėrm; it, īce; hot, ōpen, ôrder; oil; out; cup, pùt, rüle; child; long; thin; /ŦH/ for then; /zh/ for measure; /u/ or /ə/ represents /a/ in about, /e/ in taken, /i/ in pencil, /o/ in lemon, and /u/ in circus.

Grasslands of the World

Small areas of grass can be found in many places, including, perhaps, your back yard; but when geographers speak of *grasslands*, they are talking about large regions that were once covered with wild grass. These natural grasslands can be found on every continent except Antarctica.

In North America, the grasslands are called the Great Plains. They stretch from Canada to Texas in the center of the continent. In South America, the *llanos* (yä' nōs) are north and south of the Amazon rain forest, while the *pampas* are further south, in Argentina and Uruguay. In Africa, the savanna winds around the outside of the rain forests near the equator. In South Africa, the treeless grassland was named the *veld* by Dutch settlers. In Europe and Asia the grasslands are called the *steppes*, and stretch across the center of the two continents. In Australia, the grasslands circle the central desert.

Grasslands can be divided into three different types: prairie, steppes, and savanna. Prairie comes from the French word for meadow. It was used by the French explorers who first saw the tall grasses of the Great Plains. Prairie grass is often taller than a man's waist.

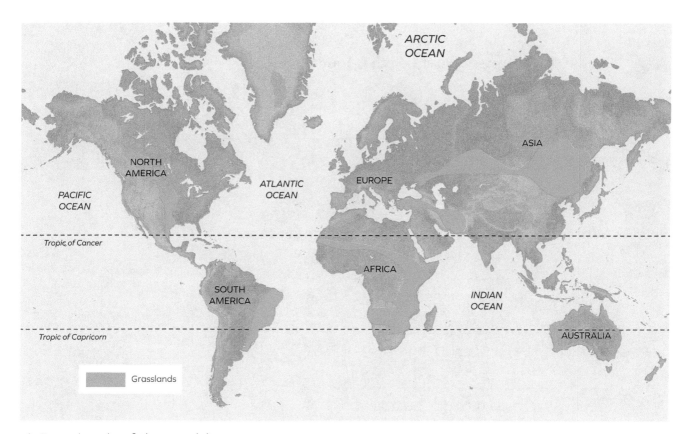

| Grasslands of the world

Steppes have shorter grass than prairies because they get less rain. Grass on the steppes may grow in little bunches instead of being spread out evenly like a lawn. Both steppes and prairies have hot summers and cold winters. The western side of the Great Plains, near the rain shadow of the Rocky Mountains, is steppes, not prairie.

Savanna is grassland in the tropics, the land between the Tropics of Cancer and Capricorn, around the equator. Savannas do not have much change in temperature during the year, but they do have a great change in rainfall. Savannas have a wet and a dry season. The plants must be able to live without water for months during the dry season and live through heavy rains in the wet season. Most of the savanna on earth is in Africa, but there is some in South America and Australia, too.

The names of the grasslands can be confusing. People often call the grasslands of Eurasia *the Steppes*, and those in North America, *the Prairie*. They are using the words as a name for the place, not as a way to describe the type of grass there. This LIFEPAC will use *prairie* and *steppes* to describe a type of grassland, not a specific place.

Name the continent where each is found.

1.1   veld _____

1.2   pampas _____

1.3   Great Plains _____

Write the correct word to complete each sentence.

1.4   _____ is a type of grassland in the tropics, which has a wet and a dry season.

1.5   _____ is a type of grassland that has tall grass, hot summers, and cold winters.

1.6   _____ is a type of grassland that has short grass because it gets little rain, but also has hot summers and cold winters.

1.7   More than half of all the crops people grow for food are _____ .

| A lioness on a savanna in Africa

Grasslands often have rich, **fertile** soil. Less rain falls on grasslands than in the forests which can wash out the minerals that helps plants grow. Also, the grasses die and pile up quickly, then decompose to fertilize the soil. The grasslands often have a thick layer of very, very good black soil from the dead grass.

The dead grass and roots from the living grass make a thick mat on top of the ground called "sod." Sod is difficult to cut through and sticks together so well that people can build with it. Many of the early settlers on the Great Plains lived in sod houses. The thick sod blocks kept the house warm in the winter and cool in the summer.

There are usually very few trees on the grasslands, because they need more water than grass does. Savannas do have special trees scattered here and there. In other grasslands, trees are found along rivers or lakes or where people have planted them.

Grass grows well even in dry places because it grows so fast. It can quickly sprout up when there is rain and die when there isn't, leaving seeds for the next time. Trees need to grow for many years to produce seeds.

The savanna is unusual because it gets a great deal of rain during the wet season. Trees that can store up water or send down deep roots can live on the savanna. Savannas usually have trees spread out among the grass, looking as if somebody dropped them in the wrong place.

Surprisingly, fire is very helpful to grasslands. It burns off dead grass on top of the sod, which allows sunlight and rain to reach the ground so new grass can grow. The ash also fertilizes the soil. Fires bring new grass to the land for the animals that live there to eat.

Many kinds of large grass-eating animals live on the grasslands. Bison, called buffaloes, live on the Great Plains. Elephants, zebras, and wildebeests (wil' də bēsts) live on the African savannas. The grasslands that can feed these large animals can also feed their domestic cousins. Cattle are raised for food on all the great grasslands of the world.

Smaller plant-eaters like deer and antelope also live on the grasslands. The pronghorn antelope in North America, the saiga in Eurasia, and the impala of Africa are all swift-running creatures of the plains. They can run within minutes of when they are born. They use their speed over the flat land to escape predators.

The other major kind of grass-eater escapes in a different way, by going underground. Ground squirrels, gophers, mice, and rabbits live in burrows under the ground, where they flee for safety. These small rodents usually outnumber the bigger **herbivores**. They live together in large groups. Prairie dogs of the Great Plains are famous for their large group homes. They have underground towns that go for miles.

The meat-eaters of the grasslands must be swift, strong, or clever to catch prey on flat land, where they are easily seen. The wolves of North America hunt in groups to encircle, run down, and capture an animal. Lions in Africa do the same. Cheetahs rely on their speed to catch their prey. Foxes and owls eat the unwary rodents they catch outside their underground homes.

| A group of blue wildebeests grazing

Write *true* or *false* on the blank.

1.8	_____	Grasslands often have rich soil.
1.9	_____	Sod is the thin tops of the grass on a prairie.
1.10	_____	Savannas have more trees than most grasslands.
1.11	_____	Grasslands are too dry for most trees.
1.12	_____	Bison live on the steppes of Eurasia.
1.13	_____	There are many kinds of rodents in the grasslands.
1.14	_____	Rodents usually live alone to protect themselves.
1.15	_____	The saiga live on the steppes of Eurasia.
1.16	_____	Cattle are never raised on the grasslands.
1.17	_____	Fires help wild grasslands.

Breadbasket of Europe

Ukraine is the second largest country in Europe. It is called the "breadbasket of Europe" because of its rich farmland. It is located north of the Black Sea and the Sea of Azov in eastern Europe. Only Russia is bigger than Ukraine on the continent.

Most of Ukraine is a large flat plain called the steppes. The Carpathian (kär pā′ thē ən) Mountains do cross the southwest (down and left, on the map) corner of the country. A large peninsula, called the Crimea, sticks out into the Black Sea and the Sea of Azov in the south. The Strait of Kerch connects the Sea of Azov to the Black Sea. The Crimean Mountains run across the bottom of this peninsula. But most of the rest of the country is plains that tilt down towards the Black Sea.

The Black Sea is part of an ocean, not a lake. It connects with the Mediterranean Sea through the Bosporus Strait. This allows ocean ships to reach the southern ports of Ukraine.

Ukraine's main seaport is the city of Odessa. Its name comes from *Odesos*, a Greek colony that was built there hundreds of years before the birth of Christ. The city is both a manufacturing and trade center.

The capital of Ukraine is Kiev, on the Dnepr (nē' pər) River. The Dnepr is the third-longest river in Europe. Its source is in the hills of western Russia. It flows through Belarus (bel ə rüs') and Ukraine on its way to the Black Sea. The river is navigable for most of its length. It is an important trade route for Ukraine and its neighbors.

Ukraine is at the same latitude as the border between the U.S. and Canada. It has warm summers and cold winters which is one of the best climates for crops. Kiev is usually about 21° F (-6° C) in January and 67° F (19°) in July. The coast of the Black Sea and the Crimean Peninsula have a much warmer climate because they are exposed to the warm waters of the Black Sea.

More than half of the land in Ukraine is arable. (Less than one fourth of the U.S. is arable.) The rich dark soil, called *chernozem*, makes it one of the best farmlands in the world.

Ukraine is the world's leading producer of sugar beets. It is also an important producer of wheat. Farmers also grow barley, corn, potatoes, vegetables, fruit, sunflowers, **flax**,

| Ukraine and neighboring countries

and tobacco. The pasture lands feed cattle for both beef and **dairy** products. The farmers also raise pigs, sheep, and chickens. In all, farming employs about one out of every four people in the country.

Ukraine is also blessed with a great many mineral resources. In addition to having large reserves of coal and iron ore, it also has deposits of **manganese**, **bauxite**, **titanium**, **uranium**, marble, sulphur, nickel, gold, and precious stones. Ukraine has some natural gas, but it does not have much oil for fuel. It must import most of its oil and some of its natural gas from Russia.

Complete these map activities.

1.18 If the Sea of Azov was not called a "sea," what else could it be?

_____

1.19 What country is east of Ukraine? _____

1.20 Name two countries that are west of Ukraine.

_____

1.21 What is the name of the peninsula that separates the Black Sea and

the Sea of Azov? _____

1.22 The Strait of Kerch connects what two bodies of water?

_____

Complete these items.

1.23 What is Ukraine called? _____

1.24 What are the flat plains of Ukraine called? _____

1.25 Name the two mountain ranges in Ukraine.

_____

1.26 What is the capital of Ukraine? _____

1.27 What is the third-longest river in Europe? _____

1.28 Which has a warmer climate, Kiev or Crimea? _____

1.29 What is the name of Ukraine's main seaport? _____

1.30 What is the black, rich soil of Ukraine called? _____

1.31 Name Ukraine's two most important crops.

_____

1.32 Circle the Ukrainian mineral resources.

uranium	iron ore	nickel
silver	salt	copper
chromium	manganese	titanium

Conquered Borderland

The ancient Roman Empire that conquered most of Europe during the time of Christ reached as far north and east as the Ukraine. After the Romans left, people called *Slavs* came and settled in the area. The word "Ukraine" comes from a Slavic word that means borderland. Besides being the old border of the Roman Empire, Ukraine was the border of the Slavic lands.

| Flag of Ukraine

The Slavic people set up a kingdom at the city of Kiev called *Kievan Rus'* in the A.D. 800s. This kingdom made much of its money by trading with the Byzantine Empire, whose capital was Constantinople (Istanbul).

One of the rulers of Kievan Rus', Vladimir the Great, became a Christian in A.D. 988. He made his entire kingdom become Christian also. (The Slavs had worshiped idols before that.) Vladimir chose a kind of Christianity called *Eastern Orthodox*, which will be discussed later in this section.

Kievan Rus' eventually fell apart, and the land was invaded by the Tartars (tär tərs) from the east in 1240. *Tartar* was the name given to the Mongol nomads of the Gobi Desert who conquered most of Asia and part of Europe in the 1200s. They were cruel, violent people who terrified the Europeans. Eventually, around 1300, they withdrew, and Ukraine was taken over first by Lithuania and then Poland.

The Poles, who came to power in 1569, forced the **peasants** to become **serfs**. The Poles also tried to force the people to become Roman Catholic, the main church in Poland even today. Some of the churches agreed and formed the Ukrainian Catholic Church, which will also be covered later in this section.

The Ukrainian peasants fought back by escaping and making their homes out in the wilderness. They elected their own leaders and learned to fight. They became excellent soldiers known as *Cossacks*. (The word means *free person* in Turkish.) They were often hired by the Russians and Poles to fight the Tartars and other enemies.

Finally, however, the harsh rule of the Poles made the serfs and the Cossacks revolt. They defeated the Poles and

| A Russian Cossack on horseback

created a new nation named Ukraine under Cossack leadership in 1648. The Cossacks then became allies with Russia (whose people are also Slavs) to hold off the Poles, who were trying to recapture the land. The Russians used the alliance to take over Ukraine themselves in 1657. The Cossacks then sought help from the Poles, but nothing worked. In the end, Poland and Russia divided Ukraine up between themselves.

The Cossacks kept fighting, but they never again were able to free their country. At the end of the 1700s, the Russian czar (ruler) attacked the Cossacks and destroyed them. Russia then took over almost all of Ukraine in 1781. Only one small part of what is now Ukraine was not under Russian rule. That one area, called Galacia, was ruled by Austria. The rest of Ukraine was forced to give up its language and culture and become more Russian, as the czar wanted.

The Russian government was very **autocratic**. The Russian people had no freedom and were treated very badly. During World War I, the people of Russia revolted and created a **communist** government under a man named Vladimir Lenin. When the revolt occurred in 1917, Ukraine declared its independence and set up its own government.

The new freedom did not last, however. Communists in Ukraine fought with the new government and other nearby countries that wanted the rich land. In the end, the communists won, and in 1922 most of Ukraine became part of the newly-formed *Union of Soviet Socialist Republics (USSR)*. Supposedly that meant that Ukraine was a "republic" equal to Russia in the "Union." In fact, Ukraine had no equality and no freedom at all. Ukraine was subject to yet another cruel master.

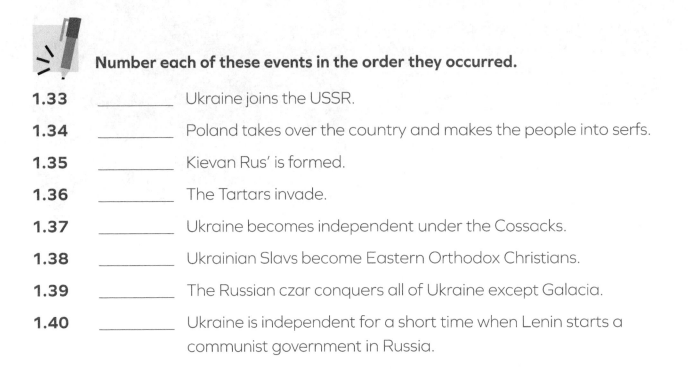

Number each of these events in the order they occurred.

1.33 _____ Ukraine joins the USSR.

1.34 _____ Poland takes over the country and makes the people into serfs.

1.35 _____ Kievan Rus' is formed.

1.36 _____ The Tartars invade.

1.37 _____ Ukraine becomes independent under the Cossacks.

1.38 _____ Ukrainian Slavs become Eastern Orthodox Christians.

1.39 _____ The Russian czar conquers all of Ukraine except Galacia.

1.40 _____ Ukraine is independent for a short time when Lenin starts a communist government in Russia.

The communists who took over in Russia believed that the government should own everything and use it for the people. In fact, the government owned everything and used it as the rulers wanted. Communists do not believe in any God and allow their people no freedom. People under communism are always afraid to disagree with the government because they may get arrested and put in jail.

The communists at first wanted the Ukrainian people to like their new government, so the people were allowed to use the Ukrainian language and own their own farms. However, the Ukrainian people used their freedom to oppose the communist government, so the government took away their freedom.

The Russians, under their communist ruler, Joseph Stalin, forced the people of the Ukraine to give up their farms, tools, and livestock. The land was taken away and made into huge farms called *collectives*, which hired the farmers to do the work. The farmers had no choice. They were shot or sent into exile if they tried to stop their land or things from being taken.

Stalin also forced the people to learn and use the Russian language again. The people worked to stop these changes and Stalin decided to punish them. He had all of the food taken out of the Ukraine and given to other parts of the USSR. Despite the fact the farms were growing plenty of food, millions of people died of starvation in 1932 and 1933. This was one of the largest man-made **famines** in history.

| Joseph Stalin

During World War II (1938-1945), Nazi Germany conquered Ukraine. Many of the people welcomed the change and fought against the Soviet Union with the Germans. Others fought both the Germans and the Soviets. Eventually Germany was defeated, and the Soviet Union recaptured Ukraine. After they were firmly back in control, the Soviets made Ukraine bigger by adding land they had captured during the fighting.

In the years following World War II, many kinds of factories were built in Ukraine to use the region's rich resources. Ukraine became a very important source of both food and goods for the USSR. But the lack of freedom and government control was ruining the businesses. The USSR could not supply what its people needed or wanted for their lives. Things like shoes, clothes, cars, televisions, and computers were difficult to get and did not work well.

The communists not only ran the businesses badly, they were also dishonest about the problems they had. Those two things caused a huge disaster in 1986 at Chernobyl, just north of Kiev.

Chernobyl had several plants that made electricity using **nuclear** power. Nuclear power uses invisible rays, called *radiation*, that heat things up to power machines to generate electricity. These rays are very harmful to people and must be used only in specially protected rooms.

In April of 1986, there was an explosion and fire at one of the nuclear plants in Chernobyl. Much of the deadly radiation escaped into the air. The communist government did not warn anyone! Thousands of people living nearby were **exposed** to the deadly rays. The Soviets only admitted it after the radiation spread far enough for scientists in <u>Sweden</u> to notice it.

Eventually, the entire city of Chernobyl had to be abandoned. Since radiation lasts for years and years, no one can safely live in that area for a long time. Many people have suffered and died as a result of the radiation that was leaked at Chernobyl.

Finally, in the late 1980s, a new Soviet ruler, Mikhail Gorbachev, tried to give people and businesses more freedom to make the country stronger. The Ukrainians used the new freedom to argue and vote for independence. People in the other "Republics" in the USSR did the same thing. The communists began to lose power all over the country. The Soviet Union fell apart in 1991, and Ukraine once more became an independent country.

Write *true* or *false* on the blank.

1.41 _____ The farmers were forced to give their land to the government under communist rule.

1.42 _____ The famine in Ukraine in 1932 and 1933 was man-made.

1.43 _____ The huge farms created by the communists were called collectives.

1.44 _____ Ukraine was conquered by Japan during World War II.

1.45 _____ The USSR was a well-run country that met most of the needs and wants of its people.

1.46 _____ The disaster at Chernobyl was an explosion at a nuclear power plant that released radiation into the air.

1.47 _____ Mikhail Gorbachev tried to solve the USSR's problems by ruling more strictly and allowing less freedom for the people.

1.48 _____ Ukraine became independent of the USSR in 1978.

A New, Old Country

People. Most of the people of Ukraine (almost three out of every four) are Ukrainian Slavs. There is also a large group of Russian Slavs and smaller groups of Poles, Belarussians, Moldavians, and Bulgarians.

| Interior of an Eastern Orthodox church in Russia

Ukrainian is now the language of the country. However, many of the people know Russian better than Ukrainian because they were forced to use it for so long. It may be many years before Ukrainian is once again the language of all the people.

Religions. Under communist rule, people were not allowed to believe in God. The churches that were open had to have the government's permission to remain open, and could only teach what the communists allowed. The people who went to those churches usually could not get good jobs and could be sent to jail if they taught others about their faith. If people went to a secret church that did not have government permission (many churches refused to get it), they could be arrested, killed, or sent to prison.

In spite of the **persecution**, the churches of the Ukraine kept going under communism and now are growing rapidly. Most of the people are part of the Eastern Orthodox Church. This is a type of Christian church that is very different from what we are used to in European and American Christianity. The differences come from the time of the Roman Empire.

The Roman Empire split into two parts at the end of the A.D. 300s. The Roman Catholic Church became the religion of the western half, while the Eastern Orthodox Church became the religion of the eastern half, or Byzantine Empire. The two churches think differently about God, have different services, and use different dates for celebrating Christian holidays.

Eastern Orthodox worship is very beautiful. The priests wear rich, colorful robes. The service uses long prayers and hymns, often from scripture. The church itself is covered with *icons*, bright pictures of Jesus, Mary, and faithful Christians of the past. It is intended to remind the people of the beauty and majesty of God.

Eastern Orthodox churches are divided into groups, each with its own *patriarch* or leader. No one patriarch is more important than the others. They have no pope, as the Roman Catholic church does. The churches in a nation usually are one group. That makes them the church of just that nation. So, Eastern Orthodox Churches usually work with the government and are part of the national culture. Under the communists the Ukrainian church was forced to become part of the <u>Russian</u> Orthodox Church. Today though, it is again the <u>Ukrainian</u> Orthodox Church.

The Ukraine also has another church, called the Ukrainian Catholic Church. It came from the days when Poland ruled the land. The churches of that time agreed to accept the pope as their spiritual ruler. This church today uses the Eastern Orthodox service and ways, but accepts the pope, who heads the Catholic Church, as their head also.

Culture. The people of Ukraine are well known for their handmade crafts. The most famous are their Easter eggs, called *pysanky*. A design is drawn on the egg in wax, then the egg is dipped in a colored dye. The wax keeps the color off parts of the egg. More designs are put on, and the egg is dipped in more colors. In the end, the egg is covered with beautiful designs in many colors.

Another craft in Ukraine is **embroidery**. The people of Ukraine wear clothes just like Americans, except for special occasions. On special occasions, they wear costumes decorated with embroidery. It takes hours and hours of careful sewing to make their gaily decorated shirts, skirts, vests, and scarves.

Ukrainian people love music. Groups that sing and dance are very popular. Ukrainians have their own musical instrument, called a *bandura*, that is used to play old Ukrainian songs. A bandura is a large stringed instrument like a lute, that was used by blind singers to perform the songs of Ukraine's past.

| Ukrainian Easter eggs

The people of Ukraine also like modern pastimes. Soccer is the most popular sport in the country, as it is in much of Europe. The people also like to play chess and take vacations on the warm beaches of the Crimea.

Problems. Ukrainian people do not remember ever being free. They had never voted for their government officials, owned their own land, or run their own businesses before 1991. Today they are trying to learn to do all of these things.

Their government is elected by the people, but most of the new leaders used to be communists. Those leaders are used to being able to give any orders they want and get all kinds of money or special treatment from their jobs. They have never learned how to help people, because what the people wanted never used to matter!

The government still owns most of the businesses, factories, mines, and farms. It is difficult for the Ukrainians to know how to change to owning and running these things themselves. The government does not like to give up its control. Many of the factories cannot produce goods that are made well enough for people to want to buy them. That means that many of the factories are forced to close, and then people lose their jobs. Thus, there are many problems Ukraine faces from becoming free again. However, the people prefer to solve their own problems in their new, old country.

Unscramble the letters to find the word to complete each sentence.

1.49 Most of the people of the Ukraine are Ukrainian (vlass) _____ .

1.50 The most famous Ukrainian handcraft is (synpkay) _____ .

1.51 Leaders in the Eastern Orthodox Church are called (trripscaha)

_____ .

1.52 A (darbanu) _____ is a large Ukrainian musical instrument with strings.

1.53 In Roman times, Eastern Orthodoxy was the religion of the (zinntebya)

_____ Empire.

Write *true* or *false* on the blank.

1.54 _____ Many of the people of Ukraine speak Russian.

1.55 _____ Eastern Orthodox services are very colorful and beautiful.

1.56 _____ Orthodox churches are decorated with icons.

1.57 _____ The Ukrainian Catholic Church services are just like those in the Roman Catholic Church.

1.58 _____ It has been difficult for Ukraine to change from a communist country to a free country.

1.59 _____ The churches were all destroyed by the Soviets and had to completely begin again in 1991.

Review the material in this section to prepare for the Self Test. The Self Test will check your understanding of this section. Any items you miss on this test will show you what areas you will need to restudy in order to prepare for the unit test.

SELF TEST 1

Choose the correct word from the list to complete each sentence (3 points each answer).

prairie	steppe	savanna	Pampas
icon	chernozem	serf	pysanky
communist	collective		

1.01 The rich, black soil of Ukraine is called _____ .

1.02 The _____ are the grasslands of Argentina and Uruguay.

1.03 Russia's government became _____ after a revolt in 1917.

1.04 An _____ is an Eastern Orthodox picture of Jesus or a faithful Christian.

1.05 A _____ is a dry grassland with short grass.

1.06 _____ are Ukrainian Easter eggs.

1.07 A _____ is a type of grassland with tall, thick grass.

1.08 A _____ is a slave who is owned by the person who owns the land the slave lives on.

1.09 A _____ is a tropical grassland with a wet and dry season.

1.010 A _____ is a large farm created with land that was taken from Ukrainian farmers.

Answer these questions (10 points each answer).

1.011 Why are grasslands important to people?

_____

_____

_____

_____

1.012   Why did millions of people starve in Ukraine in 1932-33?

_____

_____

_____

_____

Match each answer with the correct letter (3 points each answer).

1.013 _____ Germany

1.014 _____ Azov

1.015 _____ Crimea

1.016 _____ Dnepr

1.017 _____ Kiev

1.018 _____ USSR

1.019 _____ Tartars

1.020 _____ Cossacks

1.021 _____ Chernobyl

1.022 _____ Eastern Orthodox

a. Mongol nomads

b. sea south of Ukraine

c. conquered Ukraine for a time during World War II

d. union Ukraine was forced to join

e. Ukrainian peasant soldiers

f. capital of Ukraine

g. place of nuclear power disaster

h. main church of Ukraine

i. river in Ukraine

j. peninsula in southern Ukraine

Write _true_ or _false_ on the blank (2 points each answer).

1.023 _____ Fire damages grasslands so nothing will grow for years.

1.024 _____ Ukraine is called the "Breadbasket of Europe."

1.025 _____ Ukraine has many mineral resources.

1.026 _____ Poland and Russia are two of the countries that have conquered Ukraine.

1.027 _____ Ukraine was never a free country until 1991.

1.028 _____ Communists are usually Roman Catholic.

1.029 _____ Ukrainian people are famous for their crafts.

1.030 _____ A leader in the Orthodox Church is called a patriarch.

1.031 _____ It is difficult for Ukraine to change from a communist to a free nation.

1.032 _____ There are grasslands on all seven continents on earth.

Teacher check:

Score _____

Initials _____

Date _____

80 / 100

2. KENYA

You will be studying Kenya in this section of the LIFEPAC. It is a country slightly smaller than Texas on the east coast of Africa right on the equator. The grassland of Kenya is called a *savanna*. Savanna is not as good for crops as grasslands in cooler climates, but the savanna of Kenya provides food for a huge number of wild animals that God designed for it. You will learn about the savanna, its problems, and how the people of Kenya have learned to live with this harsh land.

Objectives

Review these objectives. When you have completed this section, you should be able to:

3. Explain the geography, history, people, and life today in the three grassland countries.
4. Explain how the grasslands affected the countries you study.
5. Tell some of the products of the grassland countries.

Vocabulary

Study these new words. Learning the meanings of these words is a good study habit and will improve your understanding of this LIFEPAC.

city-state (sit' ē stāt'). An independent state (country) with one major city that is in control.
corrupt (kə rupt'). Influenced by bribes; dishonest.
plateau (pla tō'). A plain in the mountains or high above sea level.
population (pop yə lā' shən). The people of a city, country, or district.
rift (rift). A split; break; crack.

safari (sə fä′ rē). A journey or hunting expedition in eastern Africa.

thatch (thach). Straw, rushes, or the like, used as a roof or covering.

Pronunciation Key: h**a**t, **ā**ge, c**ã**re, f**ä**r; l**e**t, **ē**qual, t**ė**rm; **i**t, **ī**ce; h**o**t, **ō**pen, **ô**rder; **oi**l; **ou**t; c**u**p, p**ủ**t, r**ü**le; **ch**ild; lo**ng**; **th**in; /ŦH/ for **th**en; /zh/ for mea**s**ure; /u/ or /ə/ represents /a/ in **a**bout, /e/ in tak**e**n, /i/ in penc**i**l, /o/ in lem**o**n, and /u/ in circ**u**s.

Wild Savanna

| Zebras drinking from a river in Kenya

Kenya is named after Mount Kenya, which is almost right on the equator. It is the second-highest mountain in Africa. Its name in the local language is *Kere-Nyagah*, which means "mountain of whiteness." The mountain is so tall that it has snow on top. When the first European to explore the area reported it, he was laughed at by the scientists of his day. No one believed that a mountain on the equator, the hottest part of the earth, could have snow on the top!

Kenya is on the Indian Ocean. The low plains along the coast have a tropical climate. The land gets higher as you go inland. Most of the country is a high **plateau** of plains, called savanna. The best land for farming and living is not the savanna, however.

In the south and west part of Kenya is the highlands. This land is fertile, receives more rain, and (because it is high in altitude) is much cooler than the rest of the country. The capital, Nairobi (nī rō′ bē), is in the highlands. Three out of every four people in the country live in the highlands. Kenya's two most important rivers, the Tana and Galana, start in these highlands and flow to the Indian Ocean.

The Great **Rift** Valley passes through Kenya in the west. The Rift Valley is a group of steep-sided valleys that start in Syria in the Middle East (southwest Asia) and run down to Mozambique south of Kenya. The deep valleys create beautiful scenery and deep lakes.

There are two lakes worth noting in Kenya. Lake Victoria is on Kenya's west border. It is the second-biggest freshwater lake in the world (only Lake Superior in North America is bigger). It is in three countries: Kenya, Uganda, and Tanzania (tan zə nē′ ə).

Lake Turkana (formerly called Lake Rudolf), on the other hand, is a desert salt lake almost entirely in Kenya. Only a small part is in Ethiopia. Turkana is next to Kenya's only real desert, the *Chalbi*. Water comes into the lake, but never flows out. It evaporates in the desert sun, leaving salt behind.

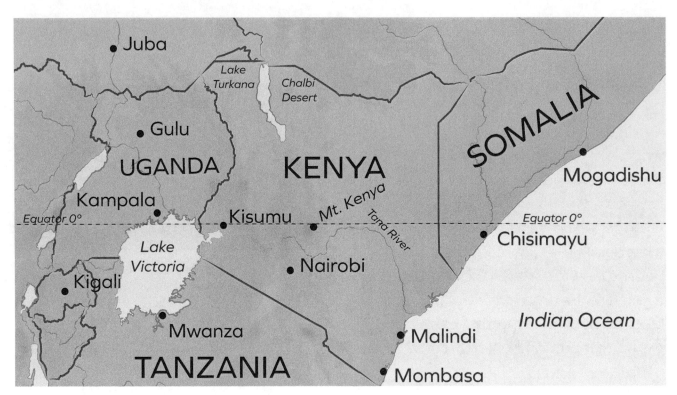

| Kenya and neighboring countries

 Complete this map activity.

2.1 Which part of Kenya is bigger: the part north of the equator or the part to the south? _____

2.2 What country is east of Kenya? _____

2.3 What is closer to the equator: Lake Turkana, Nairobi, or Lake Victoria?
_____

2.4 Name a city on the coast in Kenya. _____

Write the correct answer in the blank.

2.5 The local name for Mount Kenya is _____ , which means "mountain of whiteness."

2.6 Kenya is on the _____ Ocean.

2.7 The capital of Kenya is _____ , in the highlands.

2.8 The Great _____ runs from the Middle East through Kenya to Mozambique.

2.9 The second-largest lake in the world is Lake _____ .

2.10 Lake _____ is a salt lake in northern Kenya next to the _____ Desert.

Kenya is a country of grassland, but unlike Ukraine, it is not rich, productive land. This is a very dry grassland with poor soil. Kenya also has very few mineral resources.

Three-fourths of the country is covered with plains. They are low in altitude along the coast, but get higher further inland, making a large plateau. The part east of Lake Turkana is the only true desert, but the rest can be very close to desert.

Savannas usually get between 4 and 16 inches (100 to 400 mm) of rain in a year. An area is often called a desert if it gets 10 inches (250 mm) or less of rain in a year. These lands, however, are called savanna because of the type of plants that live there and how they get their rain. Savannas have a wet and dry season. During the wet season it can rain hard for long periods of time then not rain at all in the dry season.

Savannas that have more rain often have many trees spaced out across their plains.

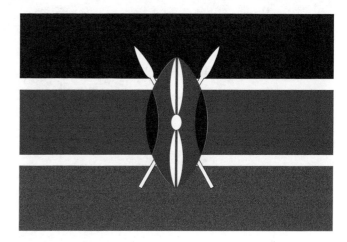

| Flag of Kenya

These trees have deep roots or store water as do desert plants, to live through the dry season. Drier savannas will have only grass, and it will be spread out in clumps here and there.

The dry land will not grow crops well, but it is home to many kinds of wild animals. Kenya has special parks where the animals are protected from hunters. One park, Tsavo Reserve, is about the size of the state of Massachusetts! People come from all over the world to go on photo **safaris** in Kenya's parks.

The people come to Kenya on safari to see animals like the lion, giraffe, wildebeest, rhinoceros, zebra, leopard, elephant, cheetah, and antelope. These animals live on the savanna grasslands.

The wild herbivores move as they eat, never staying in one spot and eating all the grass there. God designed the animals to make the best use of the grass and leave plenty for the others. People also raise cattle on the savanna. These animals are kept in one place and often eat up all of the grass there.

| Elephants in Tsavo Reserve in Kenya

Write *true* or *false* on the blank.

2.11   _____   Kenya is rich in mineral resources.

2.12   _____   Savanna is not good crop land.

2.13   _____   Savannas can get as little rain as a desert.

2.14   _____   Rain on the savanna comes any time of the year.

2.15   _____   Kenya's wild animals are protected in special parks.

2.16   _____   Only a very few animals can live on the dry savannas of Kenya.

Complete this activity.

2.17   Pretend you are going on a photo safari in Kenya. Write a paragraph about the animal you most want to see and what you want to see it doing. (Use an encyclopedia if you need help.) Then draw a picture of a scene you would like to photograph on your safari.

Kenya's Story

Along the east coast of Africa, including Kenya, many cities traded with the Middle East and Europe from before the time of Christ. The Greeks, Romans, and Arabs all traded for gold, ivory, animal skins, salt, and slaves with the coastal cities. The cities got these goods by trading with the tribes of central Africa.

The trade grew and the port cities became small, independent countries called **city-states**. Mombasa and Malindi were important city-states in this trade. Arab merchants settled in the cities and controlled much of the trade in the A.D. 700s. They mixed with the local people and created a culture called *Swahili*, a combination of the Arab and the black African *Bantu* cultures.

The Portuguese sailed around Africa to reach India in 1498. They found these rich trading cities all along the coast on their route. The Portuguese took over the trade for about a hundred years, using their military power. They captured Mombasa in the 1500s, built a huge fort there, and named it Fort Jesus.

Eventually, however, the Portuguese lost control of the trade in the 1600s as the British and Dutch took over. The British preferred to trade with local rulers who gave them special deals. They did not want the problems of running the countries themselves, so the Arabs' city-states became independent again.

In the 1800s, the Sultan of Oman (on the Arabian Peninsula) conquered all of the coastal cities and began building plantations to grow crops for trade. To get workers for his land, he increased the slave trade along the coast. Thousands of Africans were captured by other tribes and sold to work the plantations along the coast and on the islands next to it.

The British, however, had begun to fight against slavery by the 1800s. Missionaries and godly men in England were working to stop this horrible trade. The British government forced the sultan to restrict the trade in the 1850s. Finally, fearing that the British might use slavery as a reason to take over his lands, the sultan ended the trade altogether in 1873.

| Fort Jesus in Mombasa, Kenya

Britain was slowly becoming more interested in controlling Kenya itself. At that time, European countries were taking over other parts of the world as colonies to get resources they needed like wood, cotton, sugar, and tea. Many countries were trying to claim parts of Africa, and their leaders were afraid of a war over the continent. Finally, at the Berlin Conference in 1884, the Europeans peacefully divided Africa among themselves. Britain took Kenya.

Answer these questions.

2.18 What people traded with the east coast cities before the Portuguese came?

_____

2.19 What were the two important trading city-states in Kenya?

_____

2.20 What was the culture created by the mixing of Arab and Bantu?

_____

2.21 How long did the Portuguese control the east coast trade?

_____

2.22 Who conquered the east coast city-states in the 1800s?

_____

2.23 What trade were the British trying to stop in the 1800s?

_____

2.24 What happened to Africa at the Berlin Conference in 1884?

_____

_____

_____

The main reason the British wanted Kenya was Lake Victoria. It is the source of the Nile River, which flows through Egypt. Britain controlled Egypt and did not want anyone else to be able to block the river that brings water and life to that country.

Britain's real control of Kenya began in 1896, when the government decided to build a railroad to connect Lake Victoria with the city of Mombasa. The government had to defeat the African ethnic groups that did not want the railroad running across their land. Stations had to be built and workers protected, so British officials and troops took control of the land.

The railroad opened Kenya to white settlers, who discovered the fine farmland of the highlands. Thousands of Indian workers who came to build the railroad also stayed to set up businesses. The city of Nairobi began as a station on the rail line. The government quickly agreed to take all land the black Africans were not using and to keep the best farmland only for white settlers.

Missionaries, in the meantime, began to educate the Kenyan people. As they became better educated, the Kenyans began to argue for freedom and their own right to have the good farmland. The government, controlled by the white settlers, would not listen.

In the 1950s, the Kikuyu people fought to get more land. It was called the Mau Mau Revolt. The white government overreacted. Thousands of Kikuyu were killed or arrested. An important Kikuyu leader named Jomo Kenyatta was sent to jail for seven years, even though it was not proven that he had committed a crime.

| Lake Victoria at dawn

HISTORY & GEOGRAPHY 404

LIFEPAC TEST

NAME _____

DATE _____

SCORE _____

HISTORY & GEOGRAPHY 404: LIFEPAC TEST

Put a *U* on the line if the statement is about Ukraine, a *K* if it is about Kenya, and an *A* for Argentina (3 points each answer).

1. _____ used to be communist

2. _____ the main religion is Eastern Orthodox

3. _____ the people are mostly Slavic

4. _____ Lake Victoria and Lake Turkana

5. _____ on the equator

6. _____ the military has taken over the government many times

7. _____ the grassland is savanna

8. _____ the grassland is called the Pampas

9. _____ Patagonia and Gran Chaco

10. _____ Sea of Azov and Dnepr River

11. _____ tourists come to see the lions, elephants, and giraffes

12. _____ one-third of the people live in the capital

13. _____ part of the British Commonwealth of Nations

14. _____ in Europe

15. _____ in South America

16. _____ in Africa

17. _____ mainly south of the Tropic of Capricorn

18. _____ used to be one of the ten richest countries in the world

19. _____ the best farmland is <u>not</u> the grassland

20. _____ millions of people died in a man-made famine in 1932-33

Choose the correct answer from the list to complete each sentence (2 points each answer).

Kiev	Carpathian	Crimea	Swahili
Black	Indian	Nairobi	Perón
Buenos Aires	Tierra del Fuego		

21. _____ is an island south of Argentina.

22. The _____ Sea is south of Ukraine.

23. The _____ is a peninsula in southern Ukraine.

24. _____ is the capital of Kenya.

25. _____ was an Argentine president who spent too much money.

26. The _____ Mountains are partly in western Ukraine.

27. _____ is a language and culture that is a combination of Bantu and Arab.

28. _____ is the capital of Ukraine.

29. Kenya is on the coast of the _____ Ocean.

30. _____ is the capital of Argentina.

Write *true* or *false* on the blank (1 point each answer).

31. _____ *Los desaparecidos* are people who disappeared under Argentina's military government.

32. _____ A *gaucho* is a person who lives in Buenos Aires.

33. _____ Argentina's wealth came from its grassland.

34. _____ Kenya was a Spanish colony.

35. _____ Ukraine is the largest country in Europe.

36. _____ Very little of the food people grow is grasses.

37. _____ Steppes are wetlands with tall grass.

38. _____ Ukraine was never an independent country before 1991.

39. _____ The Cossacks were Ukrainian peasant soldiers.

40. _____ A serf is a small landowner in Kenya.

41. _____ The leaders of the Eastern Orthodox Church are called Shambas.

42. _____ The Ukranian Catholic Church obeys the Roman Catholic pope, but uses the Eastern Orthodox services.

43. _____ Ushuaia, in Argentina, is the world's southernmost town.

44. _____ The people of Kenya are divided into about 40 different ethnic groups.

45. _____ Kenya has had a one-party government during much of its history since independence.

46. _____ Ukraine is famous for its colorful Easter eggs, called *pysanky*.

47. _____ Argentina is a developing country that has never been very wealthy.

48. _____ The Mau Mau Revolt was in Ukraine in 1932.

49. _____ Kenya was forced to be a part of the USSR in 1922.

50. _____ The grasslands in Argentina, Ukraine, and Kenya are very much the same.

| Jomo Kenyatta, the first prime minister and president of Kenya

| Daniel arap Moi, president of Kenya 1978-2002

By the end of the revolt, the government realized that it needed to change its policies and work toward Kenyan independence. In 1961, the Kenyan people were finally allowed to elect their own government. In 1963, the country became an independent member of the Commonwealth of Nations. Jomo Kenyatta was the first prime minister and, later, the first president.

At the time of independence almost all of the large farms and businesses in Kenya were owned by whites, Indians, or Arabs. The black Africans, who made up most of the people, usually only had small farms and worked for the other races. Many of the whites and Asians left after independence because the new government would force them to sell their businesses to black Kenyans.

Jomo Kenyatta was the leader of Kenya until his death in 1978. During this time, Kenya became a *one-party government*. This was very common in Africa. It means that the people can elect their leaders, but they do not have any choice about who they elect. Only the person chosen by the one party (political group) can run for each job. This kind of government is usually **corrupt**, because government officials know they will not be voted out of office.

After Kenyatta's death, his vice president, Daniel arap Moi, became president. The government was corrupt, and people did not have any choices about how the country would be run. Finally, in 1991, Moi allowed people from other parties to run for government jobs. He still won the presidency in 1992, but many of the people elected to parliament came from the new parties.

Number these events in the order they occurred.

2.25 _____ White settlers start farms in the highlands.

2.26 _____ Jomo Kenyatta becomes prime minister.

2.27 _____ Kenya becomes a one-party government.

2.28 _____ The Mau Mau Revolt takes place.

2.29 _____ Daniel arap Moi becomes president.

2.30 _____ Britain builds a railroad from Mombasa to Lake Victoria.

2.31 _____ Moi allows other parties to run for office.

Answer these questions.

2.32 Why did many Whites and Asians leave after independence?

_____

_____

2.33 What did missionaries do that helped the Kenyans gain their freedom?

_____

2.34 Why did the British want Lake Victoria?

_____

_____

2.35 Why were the black people unhappy with the way the government handled the land?

_____

_____

_____

_____

Safari or Shambas

Kenya today has one of the fastest-growing **populations** in the world. More and more people are needing land for growing crops and raising livestock to feed themselves. The land the people need is also needed by Kenya's many wild animals.

Most Kenyans are poor. Farming is the most important way that they earn their living. Most of the farms are small, owned by the farmer or rented from the government. Half of everything that is grown is needed to feed the people who farm the land. The farmers grow a few *cash crops* (crops grown to sell for cash) or work another job on the side to earn money.

| A tea plantation in Kenya

The people of Kenya are divided into about 40 tribes, or ethnic groups. The largest are the Kikuyu, Kalenjin, Kamba, Luhya, and Luo. Each of these has a part of the country that is their homeland. These groups each have their own language and culture. People tend to think of themselves as Kamba or Kikuyu, not Kenyan. It is like thinking of yourself as Texan or Georgian, not American.

It is very important to the people of Kenya to have a *shambas* on their tribe's land. A shambas is a piece of land that is a Kenyan's home. Even when a Kenyan lives and works in the city, he is expected to have a shambas in the village that is his <u>real</u> home, the home of his tribe. As the number of people grows, it is becoming harder and harder for every single person to get his own land.

The land is also needed for Kenya's famous animals. Tourism is second only to farming as the most important way for people to earn money. That is the main reason the people allow the wildlife parks to continue. The poor people of Kenya who want or need land do not care about protecting the animals, but they do like to earn the money paid by tourists who come on safari.

| A cheetah mother and cub in Kenya

Besides paying for guides and hotels, tourists buy food, jewelry, carvings, and other things made by Kenyans. The people of Kenya protect the animals so the tourists will keep coming and buying. But the people also want a shambas. The choice between the safari and the shambas may become more and more difficult as there is less and less land for farming.

Answer these questions.

2.36   Pretend you are in the government of Kenya. You must decide what to do with a large piece of land. A poor tribe needs it as farmland, and a national park needs it because the animals drink from a river on the land. Who would you give it to, and why?

_____

_____

_____

_____

_____

_____

2.37   What is a shambas?

_____

_____

_____

2.38   How many ethnic groups are in Kenya? _____

Name two: _____

_____

Changing Kenya

Kenya is a part of the British Commonwealth of Nations. English is one of the official languages. The other is Swahili, the language of the port cities of the east coast. Most of the people of the country are Christian. About one out of every four follows a traditional African religion. These are religions that worship idols and spirits. A very small number of people are Muslim.

The government in Kenya has done a better job than most African governments for the people. Most African countries have ruined their businesses by trying the communist way of running things. Corrupt officials simply do not do the best for the businesses and the people who need them. The government in Kenya has allowed the people to run the businesses, and they have done a much better job.

Kenya's government also has tried hard to get the different tribes to work together and think of themselves as part of Kenya. The people who work in the government come from many different tribes, so everyone feels they are represented. Even with all this, the tribes often do not trust each other and sometimes fight, killing many people.

Most of the tribes in Kenya are learning modern ways. Even though they are not required to send their children to school, most parents do. Eight out of every ten children go through at least elementary school. Many of the children go to *harambee* schools. Harambee means "pulling together" in Swahili. These are schools the people have built where there is no government school.

| People of the Masai tribe in Kenya

A few of the tribes still keep their old ways. The Masai are a well-known tribe in Kenya that have kept their old ways. The Masai are nomads who herd cattle. Men count their wealth by how many cattle they own. They dress in colorful cloth and beads. They keep to the old ways, but the government is trying to get them to change. It takes a lot of land to feed the growing Masai herds, and the cattle damage the land by eating all the grass. No one knows how long they will be able to keep their ways, as Kenya continues to need more and more land.

Kenya is building numerous factories to make goods for its people. They import petroleum, which is made into gasoline, heating oil, and other products to sell to other countries. Mining is not very important because Kenya does not have many mineral resources.

Coffee and tea are the two largest cash crops in Kenya. These important crops are grown mostly on large plantations in the highlands. They are owned by the few wealthy people in the country. Many of the poor farmers work on the plantations to earn money for their families.

The people of Kenya like many kinds of food. All kinds of crops can be grown in the highlands, but the main food is maize (corn). It is usually cooked into a porridge with vegetables in it that is eaten every day. When the family can afford it, meat is added also. Beer and *chai* are favorite drinks. Chai is tea made very milky and sweet.

The people of Kenya love soccer, which they call football. It is played by village boys and city professionals all over the country. Track and field events are also popular. Kenya has won many medals at the Olympic Games in track and field.

Most of the people in Kenya live in the country, in small homes with **thatched** roofs. The walls of the houses are made of mud or sticks. There is no floor except the ground. More and more Kenyans are moving to the cities to find jobs. They often live in stone or cement homes there. Wealthier people live in nicer houses and apartments.

Kenya is a *developing country* which means it is a country that is changing to become more modern. Developing countries need money for factories, roads, utilities (electricity, plumbing, telephones), farm equipment, and trucks. The corruption in the government and the fighting between the different tribes makes it difficult to get that money. But Kenya still continues to build more and more of the modern things its people want. The safaris, the many shambas, and the stores will all have to find a place in Kenya.

Match these items.

2.39	_____ harambee	a.	corn
2.40	_____ Swahili	b.	nomads who herd cattle
2.41	_____ maize	c.	one of the biggest cash crops
2.42	_____ Masai	d.	one of two official Kenyan languages
2.43	_____ chai	e.	tea, milky and sweet
2.44	_____ coffee	f.	pulling together

 Write *true* or *false* on the blank.

2.45 _____ The ethnic groups in Kenya do not always get along well.

2.46 _____ Kenya's government has ruined the country's businesses by trying to run them.

2.47 _____ The people of Kenya like soccer and track events.

2.48 _____ Kenya's government has not done anything to help the tribes get along with each other.

 Review the material in this section to prepare for the Self Test. The Self Test will check your understanding of this section and will review the previous section. Any items you miss on this test will show you what areas you will need to restudy in order to prepare for the unit test.

SELF TEST 2

Put a *U* beside the items that relate to Ukraine and a *K* next to those that relate to Kenya (3 points each answer).

2.01 _____ Eastern Orthodox   **2.02** _____ steppes

2.03 _____ savanna   **2.04** _____ Great Rift Valley

2.05 _____ Sea of Azov   **2.06** _____ Indian Ocean

2.07 _____ shambas   **2.08** _____ Black Sea

2.09 _____ slavic people   **2.010** _____ on the equator

Choose the correct word from the list to complete each sentence (3 points each answer).

Kiev	Nairobi	Cossacks	Chalbi
Mombasa	Crimea	Uganda	Russia
Dnepr	Swahili		

2.011 _____ is the capital of Kenya.

2.012 _____ is a port city in Kenya that was one of the old trading city-states of Africa's east coast.

2.013 The _____ is a peninsula in Ukraine.

2.014 The _____ River in Ukraine is the third-longest river in Europe.

2.015 _____ was the culture of the east coast city-states and is one of the official Kenyan languages.

2.016 _____ is a country next to Kenya.

2.017 _____ is a country next to Ukraine.

2.018 _____ is the capital of Ukraine.

2.019 _____ were Ukrainian peasant soldiers.

2.020 The _____ Desert is in Kenya near Lake Turkana.

Answer these questions (4 points each answer).

2.021 What is Kenya named for?

_____

2.022 Why did the British want Lake Victoria?

_____

2.023 Why do so many tourists come to Kenya?

_____

2.024 What trade did the British work to end in Africa in the 1800s?

_____

2.025 Why are grasslands important to people? _____

_____

Write *true* or *false* on the blank (2 points each answer).

2.026 _____ A prairie is a grassland with short grass growing in clumps here and there.

2.027 _____ People in Ukraine starved in 1932-33 because a drought killed all the crops.

2.028 _____ The best farmland in Kenya is the savanna.

2.029 _____ Kenya has very few mineral resources.

2.030 _____ Jomo Kenyatta was the first king of Ukraine.

2.031 _____ The Kikuyu, Luo, and Kalenjin are tribes in Kenya.

2.032 _____ Kenya is a developing country.

2.033 _____ The tribes in Kenya get along very well.

2.034 _____ Ukraine has had problems changing from a communist to a free nation.

2.035 _____ A serf is not a free person.

Teacher check:

Score _____

Initials _____

Date _____

80
100

3. ARGENTINA

The grassland of Argentina is the *Pampas,* a Spanish word for plain. The Pampas is a huge prairie that spreads out across central Argentina. The endless miles of grassland, flat as a table, did not interest the early explorers. They thought it was a desert land. They were very wrong. It is, like the Great Plains and the Ukrainian steppes, some of the best farmland in the world. The Pampas is the heartland of Argentina and the source of its wealth. This section will study Argentina and the Pampas.

Objectives

Review these objectives. When you have completed this section, you should be able to:

3. Explain the geography, history, people, and life today in the three grassland countries.
4. Explain how the grasslands affected the countries you study.
5. Tell some of the products of the grassland countries.

Vocabulary

Study these new words. Learning the meanings of these words is a good study habit and will improve your understanding of this LIFEPAC.

bola (bō′ lə). A weapon made from rope tied with heavy balls at the end, used to throw at cattle and tangle their legs.

debt (det). Owing something to another, often money.

establish (e stab′ lish). To set up and keep going for a long time.

estuary (es′ chü er ē). A wide mouth of a river whose current meets the tides of the sea.

folklore (fōk′ lôr). The beliefs, stories, legends, and customs of a people.

gaucho (gou′ chō). Cowboy of the South American pampas (plains).

gourd (gôrd). The fruit of a vine whose hard, dried shell is used for cups, bowls, and other utensils.

mestizo (mes tē' zō). A South American of mixed ancestry, often Indian and Spanish.

polo (pō' lō). A game like hockey, played on horseback with long-handled mallets and a wooden ball.

poncho (pon' chō). A large piece of cloth or other material with a slit in the middle for the head to go through.

prosper (pros' pər). To be successful; have good fortune.

province (prov' ins). One of the main divisions of a country. Argentina is divided into provinces instead of into states.

smuggle (smug' əl). To bring in or take out of a country secretly and against the law.

sub-arctic (sub ärk' tik). The area around the outside the Arctic and Antarctic Circles.

suburb (sub' ėrb). A district, town, or village just outside or near a city.

terrorist (ter' ər ist). A person who uses violence and terror to get his way on some matter, especially political matters; for example, to try to overthrow a government or force it to act in a certain way.

Pronunciation Key: hat, āge, cãre, fär; let, ēqual, tėrm; it, īce; hot, ōpen, ôrder; oil; out; cup, pu̇t, rüle; child; long; thin; /ᴛH/ for then; /zh/ for measure; /u/ or /ə/ represents /a/ in about, /e/ in taken, /i/ in pencil, /o/ in lemon, and /u/ in circus.

Gran Chaco to Ushuaia

Argentina is in southeast South America. It is the second-largest country on the continent and the eighth largest in the world. The most northern part of the country is in the tropics north of the Tropic of Capricorn. The southern tip is only 600 miles (960 km) from Antarctica.

Argentina is shaped like a long, thin triangle pointed at Antarctica. West of it is the nation of Chile. The border is in the Andes Mountains that run all the way down South America's west coast. South of Argentina is the Drake Passage, that connects the Atlantic and Pacific Oceans. The Atlantic Ocean is the nation's eastern border. The northern border is shared with Paraguay, Brazil, and Uruguay.

The capital of Argentina is Buenos Aires (Spanish for "good air"). It is on the Rio de la Plata, an **estuary** at the mouth of the Paraná and Uruguay Rivers. Because the capital is an important ocean port, the estuary is regularly dredged to keep it open. Otherwise the mud and dirt from the rivers would make the water too shallow for the ships.

The Pampas, the rich grassland, spreads out around the capital. It is the source of the country's wealth. Two-thirds of the people live on the Pampas, which makes up one-fifth of the land. All the major cities are also on the Pampas.

| Argentina and neighboring countries

Wheat, sorghum, corn, soybeans, sunflower seeds, and flaxseed (which produces linseed oil for paint) are raised on the wetter eastern Pampas. The drier western Pampas, near the Andes rain shadow, is cattle-raising land. Argentina is a major exporter of grain (such as wheat) and beef products.

South of Argentina's Colorado River is Patagonia. It is a dry, windy plateau of steppes and desert. The soil is poor and the climate too dry for most crops. Some food is grown in river valleys, but most of the land is empty or used to raise sheep. Patagonia does have important oil, coal, and iron ore deposits, however.

At the southern end of Patagonia is Tierra del Fuego (Land of Fire). It is a large island and is also the name of the entire archipelago. It was named by Ferdinand Magellan when he sailed through the strait that bears his name on his trip around the world in 1520. He named it after all the fires along the coast, built by Indians trying to stay warm in the cold climate.

Tierra del Fuego is divided between Chile and Argentina. The Argentine town of Ushuaia on the main island's south coast has the distinction of being the world's most southern town. It has become an important take-off point for the people who visit Antarctica. Cape Horn, the southernmost tip of the continent, is on the Chilean island of Horn in the archipelago.

Northern Argentina is also flat. It is divided into two areas. The Gran Chaco is the flood plain of the rivers coming out of the Andes. Here dirt and gravel are slowly building up on the land. The hot land is covered with jungle, swamps, and some grassland. East of the Gran Chaco is Mesopotamia, which means "land between the rivers." In this case,

| Tierra del Fuego at sunset

| Mount Aconcagua, in the Argentine Andes

| Flag of Argentina

it is between the Paraná and Uruguay Rivers. It is a wet land of rain forest, swamps, and rolling grassland. Citrus trees and *yerbá mate*, a holly bush used to make the Argentine national drink, are grown there.

The last part of Argentina, the Andes Mountains and the piedmont, the hills at the foot of the mountains, is in the west. The tallest mountain in the Western Hemisphere, Mount Aconcagua (22,831 feet; 6,959 m) is in the Argentine Andes. Because it is in the rain shadow, the piedmont is very dry, but, the many streams coming out of the Andes allow the land to be irrigated in the better soil north of Patagonia. This is where grapes are grown for wine and export. Cattle, citrus fruit, and vegetables are also raised in the piedmont.

Argentina is a rich land that has jungles in the north and **sub-arctic** climates in the south. It has mineral resources of zinc, lead, copper, tin, and uranium, in addition to its rich croplands. From the Gran Chaco to Ushuaia the land changes much and gives Argentina a wide variety of resources.

Match these items.

3.1 _____ Ushuaia

3.2 _____ Patagonia

3.3 _____ Pampas

3.4 _____ Rio de la Plata

3.5 _____ Buenos Aires

3.6 _____ Tierra del Fuego

3.7 _____ Cape Horn

3.8 _____ Gran Chaco

3.9 _____ Mesopotamia

3.10 _____ Piedmont

3.11 _____ Aconcagua

a. estuary, Uruguay and Paraná Rivers

b. "land between the rivers"

c. hills at the foot of the Andes

d. southernmost town in the world

e. rich grasslands of Argentina

f. southernmost part of South America

g. tallest mountain in the Western Hemisphere

h. capital of Argentina

i. swamps, jungles on northern floodplain of Andes rivers

j. island and archipelago in southern Argentina and Chile

k. windy steppes/desert of the south

Riches Lost

Argentina had only a few tribes of Indians when the Spanish began taking control of South America in the 1500s. But it was not land itself that attracted the Europeans. Argentina's name comes from the Latin word for silver. That is what the early Spanish explorers hoped to find there. The fortune seekers quickly lost interest when none was discovered. Spain was far more interested in Peru and Mexico, which were rich in precious metals.

Argentina was settled slowly and without much help from Spain. The first successful Spanish settlement was in 1551 along the edge of the mountains. The settlers actually came over from Peru. The towns **established** in the piedmont traded with Peru, not with the coast.

Buenos Aires was established in 1580 on the second try (the first settlers were driven off by Indians). Spain would not even allow ships to bring goods to the port there until the mid-1700s. For many years the people of Buenos Aires did their trading by **smuggling**.

Finally, in 1776, Buenos Aires was made the capital of a new colony, called the Viceroyalty of La Plata, that covered most of southeast South America. Ships were then legally allowed to trade at the city. The city began to grow in importance.

Britain attacked Buenos Aires in 1806 and 1807, trying to take over the colony. Both times the city was successfully defended by the colonists themselves. This led them to think that they no longer needed Spanish protection. France invaded Spain in 1807 and further cut the colony off from the mother country.

Buenos Aires set up its own government in 1810. This began the long process of Argentine independence. Many of the provinces of the Viceroyalty of La Plata would not join them. Uruguay, Paraguay, and Bolivia chose independence without Argentine leadership. José de San Martin, one of the country's greatest heroes, finally convinced the Argentine **provinces** to declare independence in 1816. Then, San Martin led an army that defeated the Spanish army in Chile and Peru, freeing the region from Spanish control.

Independence did not unify the United Provinces of La Plata, as Argentina was called then. The province of Buenos Aires wanted a strong central government in their city.

| Buenos Aires, the capital of Argentina

The other provinces wanted to control themselves. The two sides fought a series of civil wars even while trying to set up a government.

From 1829-1852 a dictator named Juan Manuel de Rosas ruled the United Provinces. He was to be the first of many. He used his power to bring order by killing people who did not agree with him. Rosas also fought the "Wars of the Desert" to drive the Indians out of the Pampas and Patagonia. That opened the rich Pampas for farming and ranching.

Rosas was overthrown by the army in 1852, and a constitution was written for the country in 1853. Buenos Aires refused to join, and more civil wars were fought. Finally, though, in 1862, Buenos Aires became the capital of the nation now called Argentina.

Answer these questions.

3.12   Why were the Spanish not very interested in Argentina?

_____

_____

3.13   What year was Buenos Aires established? _____

3.14   What happened in 1776 that made Buenos Aires more important?

_____

_____

_____

3.15   What did the Argentine provinces fight about after independence?

_____

_____

3.16   Why is San Martin an Argentine hero?

_____

_____

3.17   Who was Juan Manuel de Rosas?

_____

_____

| The Pampas of Patagonia

Once Argentina finally settled the questions about its government, it began to **prosper**. The Pampas were settled by thousands of **immigrants** from Europe. The invention of refrigerated ships allowed Argentina to begin exporting fresh meat as well as grain to Europe in the late 1800s. Argentina became one of the ten richest countries in the world in the early 1900s by selling food grown on the Pampas to the industrial nations of Europe.

Argentina's wealth was based completely on crops, however, and the government was unfair. The government was controlled by the rich landowners. The people resented the fact they had no say in their own government. Changes finally allowed a fair government to be elected in 1916, but Argentina's wealth was too limited to continue.

The Great Depression began in 1929 and lasted until World War II (1939–1945). It was a time when people all over the world lost their jobs, businesses failed, and banks had to close. Europe stopped buying so much of its food from Argentina, and the country's wealth disappeared. Then, the army made matters worse. They took over the government in 1930 when the president could not fix the problems.

The wealth of Argentina has never fully returned because of problems with the government. Between 1930 and 1983 the army took over the government many times. The government, when it was elected, often made things worse rather than better.

One of the most important elected leaders who made things worse was Juan Perón. He was an officer who was part of an army takeover in 1943. He became the leader of the working people and was elected president in 1946. Argentina had more money then because people were buying more food after World War II. Perón spent the money as fast as it was earned.

Many of the things Perón did helped people, such as starting retirement pensions and inexpensive housing. Eventually, the money ran out, and Argentina was deeply in **debt**. Perón kept spending by just printing more money. That made prices go up quickly. Shoes that cost $25 one month would cost $35 next month and maybe $100 by the end of the year. People could not afford to buy the things they needed, and no one would loan the country more money. The army took over in 1955 and Perón left the country.

Terrorists began trying to force the government to do things they wanted. Perón became president again in 1973, after several presidents and army governments could not bring order and restore the country's riches. Perón failed as well and died in office in 1974. His third wife, Isabel Martinez de Perón, the vice president, became the first woman president in the Western Hemisphere. She also failed and the army overthrew her in 1976.

The new military government was determined to end the terrorism and establish an orderly country. The military began the "dirty war," one of the worst events in Argentina's history. The army began arresting, torturing, and killing anyone who did or even <u>might</u> disagree with them.

Between 10,000 and 30,000 people were arrested and murdered, and their bodies then destroyed or secretly buried. They are called *los desaparecidos*, "the disappeared ones." Even today no one knows what happened to them.

The army tried to distract the people from what they were doing by starting a war over the Falkland Islands. The islands off the coast of Argentina belong to Britain, but Argentina also claimed them. The army took over the islands in April of 1982. The British sent troops which recaptured the islands in June, killing over a thousand Argentine soldiers. This loss completely turned the people against the army, and a new president was elected in 1983.

| Penguins walking on the beach in the Falkland Islands

The new president arrested the army leaders of the "dirty war," and several of them went to prison. But that did not solve all of the country's problems. Argentina still had too much debt and prices going up too fast (called *inflation*). The new president was not able to fix these problems.

By 1997, Argentina had four free elections without an army takeover, but still the problems with debt and inflation continue. So, there is both good news and bad news for Argentina in its search to regain its lost riches. It is not a poor country, but it is very troubled.

Write *true* or *false* on the blank.

3.18 _____ Argentina's riches came mostly from its mineral wealth.

3.19 _____ Argentina was one of the ten wealthiest countries in the world in the early 1900s.

3.20 _____ The Great Depression did not change Argentina's wealth.

3.21 _____ Argentina's military has taken over the government many times since 1930.

3.22 _____ Juan Perón was a terrorist who was killed by the army.

3.23 _____ Inflation is rising prices.

3.24 _____ *Los desaparecidos* are people who left Argentina to escape from the "dirty war."

3.25 _____ The main problems in Argentina are too much debt and inflation.

3.26 _____ Argentina lost the war over the Falkland Islands to Britain.

3.27 _____ Several of the officers who led the "dirty war" went to prison.

Porteños and Gauchos

Argentina, like the United States, is a *developed* (modern) country built by immigrants. Millions of people, mainly from Spain and Italy, came to Argentina in the late 1800s and early 1900s. These immigrants built a culture that looks more like Europe than South America. Most of the people in the country are European, in fact. Only a small part of the population is **mestizo**, and even fewer are Indian.

| Argentinian Gaucho riding a wild horse to lasso bulls

Most of the people of Argentina speak Spanish and attend the Roman Catholic Church. That is typical of South America. But Argentina's people do not have a Spanish/Indian culture like so many of the other countries. Instead, they have a mixed European culture that includes British tea time, a French-looking capital, and Spanish language that sounds Italian!

The main center of culture and trade in the country is the capital, Buenos Aires. One-third of the people in Argentina live in the city or its **suburbs**, which is an unbelievably large number. The people of the city are called *porteños*, "people of the port." They think of themselves as the important part of the country.

The remainder of the population is spread out over the rest of the country. Much of it is very empty. The smaller cities of the Pampas and Piedmont are not even close to the size of Buenos Aires. Most of the Pampas is divided into *estancias*, large ranches or farms, where one family and its workers live.

The Pampas was the place where Argentina got its best-known national symbol, the **gaucho**. At first gauchos were skilled horsemen who lived on the Pampas before it was settled by ranchers. They captured wild horses and cattle to sell the hides. Their wild, free life became the subject of songs, poems, and stories all over Argentina. Like the American cowboy, they became an important part of the Argentine **folklore**.

Gauchos wear clothes that identify them, as a cowboy's hat and boots identify him. Gauchos wear loose pants, a wide-brimmed hat, a stiff belt decorated with silver, and a **poncho**. They always carry a knife. Gauchos are skilled horsemen and still often have contests on horseback, like rodeos. They capture cattle by using a lasso or a **bola** to stop the animal.

When the ranchers and farmers settled on the Pampas, they fenced in the land. That ended the gauchos' free-roaming lifestyle. Many of them began to work for the ranchers, herding cattle and training horses. Today the gauchos are usually ranch workers, but they still keep their way of dress and many of their skills.

Because of the Pampas, Argentina has always had plenty of beef. It is the national food. It is often eaten several times a day.

| Maté, Argentina's national drink

The national drink is *maté*, a tea made from the leaves of a holly bush. The tea is mixed up in a **gourd** and drunk with a silver straw.

Soccer, called *fútbol*, is the most popular sport in Argentina. The people get very excited when their teams play. Children learn to play at an early age. They dream of being professional soccer players just as American children dream of being professional football or baseball players.

Argentine people also love sports on horseback. Racing, show jumping, and **polo** are very popular. *Pato* is a popular horseback game that is played only in Argentina. Riders on horseback try to pick up a large, six-handled ball and score by putting it in a basket.

The people live in houses very much like those in America and they dress much the same also. They have TV's, cell phones, computers, and cars like Americans as well. Argentina is a modern, very European-looking country.

Argentina began building more factories and trying to use more of its mineral resources after World War II. That way the country would not have to depend completely on crops to make money. Today most of the people make their living from manufacturing or services (such as nurses, lawyers, shop owners, etc). However, most of the jobs are still based on Argentina's crops. The factories turn leather into shoes, can food, and weave wool into cloth. Services need money from the sale of crops and truckers need food to deliver for trade. Thus, the people still depend on the rich Pampas for their income, gauchos and porteños alike.

| A polo match

Match these items.

3.28 _____ mestizo

3.29 _____ estancias

3.30 _____ gaucho

3.31 _____ maté

3.32 _____ porteños

3.33 _____ fútbol

3.34 _____ pato

a. people who live in Buenos Aires

b. Argentina's national drink

c. large farms or ranches

d. soccer

e. person of Indian and Spanish blood

f. cowboy of the Pampas

g. Argentine horseback game

Write *true* or *false* on the blank.

3.35 _____ Argentina is a country of European immigrants.

3.36 _____ About one out of every ten people in Argentina lives in Buenos Aires.

3.37 _____ Gauchos are famous as great swimmers.

3.38 _____ Today Argentina has manufacturing, but much of it is based on the crops from the Pampas.

3.39 _____ Argentine people eat beef often.

3.40 _____ The gauchos' lifestyle ended when the Pampas was fenced by farmers and ranchers.

Do this word search.

3.41   Find these words. They may be up, down, diagonal, forwards or backwards.

steppe	prairie	savanna	Pampas
herbivore	Crimea	Ukraine	Dnepr
Cossack	Argentina	Kenya	Victoria
safari	shambas	Andes	Patagonia
gaucho	soccer	bola	icon
giraffe	grass	lion	wheat

```
G  S  T  E  P  P  E  T  B  O  L  A  S  T  V  G
U  R  A  B  G  I  R  A  F  F  E  R  I  S  I  A
K  E  G  H  P  A  T  A  G  O  N  I  A  D  C  U
D  N  E  P  R  Z  G  Q  A  E  I  O  R  U  T  C
A  I  K  N  A  S  S  A  R  G  D  P  G  E  O  H
N  A  E  F  J  I  C  O  N  H  J  L  E  A  R  O
A  R  N  L  S  N  V  O  P  R  S  T  N  N  I  R
C  K  Y  J  A  I  S  O  C  C  E  R  T  N  A  S
O  U  A  D  B  F  K  T  L  E  L  A  I  A  O  A
S  B  Q  R  M  S  A  R  E  I  I  N  N  V  Z  P
S  I  E  G  A  E  L  I  F  R  G  D  A  A  B  M
Z  H  N  T  H  S  R  K  O  I  C  E  D  S  P  A
G  G  A  W  S  M  Y  K  C  A  S  S  O  C  E  P
H  C  R  I  M  E  A  X  Z  R  G  E  A  R  H  Z
R  S  A  F  A  R  I  S  M  P  L  I  O  N  W  F
```

Before you take this last Self Test, you may want to do one or more of these self checks.

1. _____ Read the objectives. See if you can do them.
2. _____ Restudy the material related to any objectives that you cannot do.
3. _____ Use the **SQ3R** study procedure to review the material:
   a. **S**can the sections.
   b. **Q**uestion yourself.
   c. **R**ead to answer your questions.
   d. **R**ecite the answers to yourself.
   e. **R**eview areas you did not understand.
4. _____ Review all vocabulary, activities, and Self Tests, writing a correct answer for every wrong answer.

SELF TEST 3

Put a *U* on the line if the statement is about Ukraine, a *K* if it is about Kenya, and an *A* for Argentina (3 points each answer).

3.01 _____ on the Indian Ocean

3.02 _____ most people follow the Eastern Orthodox faith

3.03 _____ savanna

3.04 _____ became independent of Britain in 1963

3.05 _____ became independent of the Soviet Union in 1991

3.06 _____ became independent of Spain in 1810

3.07 _____ government was sometimes military, sometimes elected from 1930-1983

3.08 _____ government allowed only one party to hold office most of the time since independence

3.09 _____ government was communist for about sixty years

3.010 _____ on the Black Sea

Match these items (2 points each answer).

3.011	_____	Tierra del Fuego	a. islands Britain and Argentina fought over
3.012	_____	Patagonia	b. southernmost town in the world
3.013	_____	Pampas	
3.014	_____	Falkland	c. Argentine independence hero
3.015	_____	Ushuaia	d. mountains in Argentina
3.016	_____	San Martin	e. South America's southernmost point
3.017	_____	Perón	f. passage between Antarctica and Argentina
3.018	_____	Andes	
3.019	_____	Cape Horn	g. president who spent too much money
3.020	_____	Drake	h. fertile Argentine grassland
			i. dry, windy plateau in south Argentina
			j. island south of Argentina

Answer these questions in complete sentences (4 points each answer).

3.021 What made Argentina so rich in the early 1900s?

_____

_____

_____

3.022 Why did people starve to death in Ukraine in 1932-33?

_____

_____

_____

3.023 What are the two main problems that keep Argentina from being rich again?

_____

_____

_____

3.024 Why do Kenyans protect their wild animals?

_____

_____

_____

3.025 What is a gaucho?

_____

_____

Write *true* or *false* on the blank (1 point each answer).

3.026 _____ Kenya is named after an English explorer.

3.027 _____ There are grasslands on all the continents except Antarctica.

3.028 _____ Much of the food people grow to eat are types of grasses.

3.029 _____ Fire is helpful to a wild grassland.

3.030 _____ Argentina was settled by people who wanted to mine the large amounts of silver there.

3.031 _____ A shambas is a large ranch in Argentina.

3.032 _____ Tartars were Mongols who conquered much of Asia and east Europe.

3.033 _____ Beef is an important food in Argentina.

3.034 _____ Argentina and Ukraine are major wheat producers.

3.035 _____ *Los desaparecidos* were people who disappeared in Argentina's "dirty war."

Choose the correct word from the list to complete each sentence (2 points each answer).

Kiev	Nairobi	equator	Cossacks
Swahili	Tropic of Capricorn	Buenos Aires	Great Rift
Chernobyl	Dnepr		

3.036 _____ is the capital of Argentina.

3.037 The _____ were Ukrainian peasant soldiers.

3.038 _____ is a culture and language that is a mix of Bantu and Arab.

3.039 The _____ Valley runs from Asia down most of the east side of Africa.

3.040 The _____ is a map line that runs through Kenya.

3.041 The _____ is a map line that runs through northern Argentina.

3.042 _____ is the capital of Kenya.

3.043 The _____ River runs through Ukraine.

3.044 _____ is the capital of Ukraine.

3.045 _____ is a city that had to be abandoned due to nuclear radiation.

✔	**Teacher check:**	Initials _____	80
	Score _____	Date _____	100

Before you take the LIFEPAC Test, you may want to do one or more of these self checks.

1. _____ Read the objectives. See if you can do them.
2. _____ Restudy the material related to any objectives that you cannot do.
3. _____ Use the **SQ3R** study procedure to review the material.
4. _____ Review activities, Self Tests, and LIFEPAC vocabulary words.
5. _____ Restudy areas of weakness indicated by the last Self Test.

NOTES

NOTES